Magnetic Marketing

How to market your services
as a Coach, Consultant or Trainer

By Chantal Cornelius

Apple tree
Publications

First Published 2011
Second Edition Published 2012
Third Edition Published 2015

Copyright © Chantal Cornelius 2011
Appletree Publications
Coombe Road
Compton
Berkshire RG20 6RQ

Call: 01635 578 500

Email: Admin@Appletreeuk.com

Website: www.Appletreeuk.com

ISBN 978-0-9570913-0-6

Cover, design and typesetting by Clockwork Graphic Design

Contents

Why You Should Read This Book

Growing and developing a business is like going on a journey. You might start out with a destination in mind and a rough idea of how you're going to get there. You'll pass milestones along the way to your end point and you may lose your way along the journey. You might never reach the place you wanted to get to, or you might get there sooner than you expected.

Growing and developing my businesses has definitely been a journey – one that I'm still on. In 2000, after five years of working for other companies as their Marketing Assistant or Manager, I set up Appletree because I wanted to help more businesses. I wanted to do marketing for people who really needed some help and who appreciated the help they received. I wanted to be able to do marketing that really made a difference to the business.

Initially I started out writing copy for clients – words for press releases, articles, leaflets, brochures and websites. Then clients started to ask for ongoing marketing help, which made me realise that ad hoc marketing does not work – a theme I'll come back to in certain chapters of the book. This lead to a business that provided monthly marketing and I expanded the offering from copywriting to include a range of services. In 2005 I was writing a lot of email newsletters for clients, using a clever system for distribution, called Just Add Content (or JAC.) When the opportunity came up to buy JAC from his creator I jumped at

the chance and integrated the system into Appletree. This allowed me to significantly grow the business and build a team of staff around me. Over the years we have developed JAC and used him for many of our clients every month, for many years.

Having celebrated the 10th birthday of Appletree in August 2010, I decided it was time for another adventure and bought a networking company called Ladies That Lunch. We changed the name to Ladies and Gentlemen That Lunch. Running that company alongside Appletree gave me another way of sharing marketing advice and helping other businesses to grow and prosper.

Over the years I have come to realise that my mission is to inspire other people to succeed in their passions. Having been lucky enough to spend so many years earning a living from what I love doing, my aim is now to help as many other people to do the same thing. I see many owner managers and small businesses struggle to get going and to keep going. I see them try to do everything themselves, or not spend any money, because they do not think that they can afford to get help. There is an easier way to grow a successful business. There is no magic wand, but with some careful planning and some accurate marketing, every business that is run by someone who has a passion for what they do, can succeed, without years of struggle.

I've written this book to share some of the great secrets of effective marketing with anyone who is passionate about what they do. It is aimed specifically at coaches, consultants and trainers, and the principles can be applied to any business that provides a service or a high quality, high price product. If you work through this book, a chapter at a time, and if you take time to complete all the exercises, by the time you reach the last page, you will be holding in your hands a Marketing Plan – a route map to follow to the success of your business.

Writing this book has been a journey for me too. I knew the final destination would be what you are reading now and I knew that the milestones would be the completion of each chapter. Originally I knew when I wanted to reach the destination, and then I got delayed along the way. It took following my own advice to get me back on the right road. Along the way there have been light bulb moments for me. As I wrote the section on scheduling marketing in Chapter Eight, I realised that I had not been scheduling the marketing for either of my businesses properly – I had been too busy looking after my clients' marketing. Writing the lists of possible marketing tactics in Chapter Five reminded me of all the things I was not doing and could be. As I've written the book, I've used my own advice and ideas to improve the marketing I do for clients and my own businesses. It has even helped me to promote this book. The fact that you are reading it now means that I have done something right! Work through the chapters and you will be able to reach whatever destination you are heading for, on the journey of your business.

The SOS Marketing Plan

Early on in my marketing career, before I even thought about running my own business, I learnt a process for creating a Marketing Plan. It is this process or structure that I use now with all my clients and my own businesses. It forms the structure of this book. Why SOS? Because a way of remembering the stages is by a mnemonic – SOS TT and 4Ms.

Situation – where are you now?

Objectives – where do you want to be?

Strategy – how will you get there?

Targets – who are your ideal clients?

Tactics – what is the best marketing to do?

Money – how much does it cost?

Men And Women – who will do it?

Minutes – how long will it take?

Measurements – why should you measure?

Each of the chapters in this book deals with each stage in detail, helping you build up a comprehensive Marketing Plan.

Planning In Practice

All the way through the book I have shared real life examples of what happens when you plan your marketing. Each chapter will give you an example of how a business has put that part of the Marketing Plan into practice and how it affected the growth of their business. My thanks go to all my wonderful clients for allowing me to share their stories with you.

Now it is time for you to start your marketing journey. Turn to Chapter One to get going and enjoy the ride!

Where Are You Now?

When you first set out on a journey with a map, you need to know where you are. If you don't know where you're starting from, you can't work out the best route to your destination and you can't determine how long it's going to take you to get there.

The first thing you need to think about when you're creating a Marketing Plan for your business is where your business is now. Knowing where you are at the start of this journey will help you plan the best route to your goals. It will also help you set your goals so that you can see the distance you've got to travel between where you are now and where you want to be. You might think that you'd like to take on 100 new clients in the next twelve months, charging each one £1000 per day for consulting or coaching. However, if you've only got two clients right now and you're only charging £300 per day, you'll have a lot of work to do to reach your goal. (Of course, if that's the goal you really want to aim for, that's great and knowing your starting point will help you plan the most effective way of getting there.)

So what is your business? What resources do you have at your disposal, to deliver your services to your clients? How long have you been doing what you do and what sort of reputation and experience do you have?

You also need to think about the products and services that you currently provide and be clear on what you offer, to help you decide the best direction to take. Are you delivering what your clients actually want and are you doing what you really want to do? Is there a demand for what you want to offer or are you doing something you only think people might want?

Who are your clients (more on how to find your ideal ones in Chapter Four)? What sort of people and businesses do you work for? Where are they and why do they need your help?

Finally, what about your competitors? Do you know who your main competitors are and what they do? How much do they charge and what makes you different from them?

This chapter will guide you through all these questions in more detail, so that by the end of it, you'll be really clear on what you do now, how, why and for whom. Then you can move on to plan where want to get to and how to do it.

1

What Is Your Business?

Answer the following questions about the business and the resources you have now. Don't think yet about where you want to be – this is about where you are now and what you can currently make use of.

There are no right or wrong answers to these questions. It's all about you and you don't need to compare yourself to anyone else at this stage. Don't worry if you're quite new to business and you don't yet have a reputation or a long string of clients. This is about getting really clear on where you are now.

What resources do you have?

Describe the size and structure of your business, your current turnover and size of marketing budget – if you already have one! How many people are in your business? What external help do you have (such as a virtual assistant, a bookkeeper and other freelance support?)

....

....

....

....

What experience do you have?

How long have you been doing what you do, both within your business and before you set it up? Do you have any relevant qualifications or accreditations? What do you specialise in?

....

....

....

....

....

What sort of reputation do you have?

How well known are you in your business community or in your field? Have people heard of you? Can you find yourself on the internet? (If you're not sure, Google your name and see what comes up!)

....

....

....

....

What Products Or Services Do You Provide?

The next areas to describe in this section of your Marketing Plan are your products and services – the things you deliver to your clients, for which they pay.

A note on the differences between products and services, in case you're not sure:

A Product is something:

• Tangible that can be picked up, touched, held and looked at

• That can be directly compared to a similar product

• Like a book, a fact sheet that can be printed, or a CD.

A Service is something:

• Intangible that can't be picked up, touched, held or looked at

• That can't be directly compared to something else in terms of how it looks, feels or sounds

• Like a coaching session, a staff audit or a management review.

Many consultants and coaches only sell services to their clients – you sell yourself and your time. Some also sell a range of products such as books, CDs or DVDs.

Whether you sell products or services, when you describe them, you need to be really specific. If you're an HR Consultant, don't just write down that you provide HR consulting services. How do you deliver that consulting? Is it through one to one sessions, group meetings, monthly advice on the phone or some other way? Do you work on a retainer or on an ad hoc basis? Do you package your services, for instance in a series of 10 coaching calls? However you do it, you need to list them all!

How much do you charge for your products and services? Use the space below to describe, in plenty of detail, all your products and services, how much they cost and how you deliver what you do.

1

....

....

....

....

....

....

....

....

....

....

....

Who Are Your Clients?

In Chapter Four we'll look at how to work out who your ideal clients are – the people you really want to work with. For now, in this section, describe your current clients.

Who are they? What sort of people are they? Describe them in terms of age and gender if you work with consumers and individuals. Where do they work and what do they do? How much do they earn? What issues are they struggling with, that bring them to your door? How many of these clients do you have?

If you work with businesses, describe them in terms of size (of turnover, staff or both), the type of business they are in, their specialty, their clients and their location. What issues do they face that you help them with? How many of these businesses do you work with?

Describe your current clients in the space below. This exercise is a useful way of starting to segment your clients. For instance, you might work with companies with 5 to 500 employees. Do you notice any similarities between the ones with 5-50 employees, those with 51-100 employees and the others with 101-500 employees? They probably have different needs, so you will need to work with them differently and provide specific services. Be aware of this as you start describing them.

....

....

....

....

....

....

....

What's Your Emotional USP?

Do you have a USP – a Unique Selling Point? Some businesses have a USP that they use to show how they're totally different from others. Most consultants and coaches don't have just one thing that makes them different, but if you do, then make sure you tell people what it is.

Do you have an emotional USP?

Most people buy because they want something, not because they need it. They buy on emotion. There are six human emotional needs first articulated by Tony Robbins. These have been further developed by Nikki Burns, Entrepreneur and Business Advisor, into a structure for formulating the emotional USP for your business. This helps you to establish and articulate the key reason why people will buy from you. To find out more about Nikki Burns visit www.nikkiburns.net.

The six emotional needs are listed below with a description of an associated business USP driven by emotion:

- Certainty – because they know you'll get the job done. You provide security and consistency

- Contribution – because they know you'll help them make a significant contribution through their business

- Connection – because they know you'll be able to connect them with the people they need

- Growth – because they know you'll help their business to grow. They want continual personal and business development

- Variety – because they know you'll bring them the variety they want. They prefer uncertainty

- Significance – because they know you'll help them feel valued. They want to feel important and needed.

At Appletree, my marketing company, our emotional USP is certainty. Our clients work with us because they know we'll get their marketing done for them, on time, on budget and without them having to worry about it. We use this in our marketing messages, to tell prospective clients that they can trust us to do their marketing and get them new clients.

What's your emotional USP?

....

....

....

....

....

1

Who Are Your Competitors?

The final aspect of your business that you need to think about in this section, to help you work out where you are now, is your competition.

Every business has competitors and they can take two different forms – direct and indirect. What's the difference?

Direct competitors do exactly what you do. If you're a coach who specialises in helping people lose weight, your direct competitors are other coaches who help people to lose weight. They don't need to specialise in doing it – as long as it's one of the things they do, then they are a direct competitor.

Indirect competitors are people to whom your clients can go to for similar help. Using the weight loss coach as the example again, indirect competitors include personal trainers, gyms and sports clubs that people can go to, in order to lose weight. If someone else helps people achieve the same end result, but in a different way, they are an indirect competitor.

You need to consider your indirect competition as carefully as your direct competition. Just because there are no other financial consultants listed in your area in the Yellow Pages, does not mean that there's no local competition. Look at the number of banks, accountants, bookkeepers to whom your clients might turn for financial advice.

So do you know who your main competitors are and what they do? How much do they charge? What area do they cover? Depending on what you do and the area you cover, you don't need to know every detail about every single competitor for miles around – but you do need an idea of what you're up against. Search the internet for people who do what you do and see who comes up.

The key thing to think about when comparing your business to your competitors is what makes you different. What makes you stand out from them? Why would someone come to you instead of going somewhere else?

Describe your competitors here:

....

....

....

....

....

....

....

....

Summary

Now that you've worked through Chapter One, you should be really clear on exactly what your business does, the products and services your provide, who you provide them for and what your competitors are up to.

Chapter Two will help you take that information and set your short, medium and long term goals for the growth of your business. This is where you get to decide where you want to go!

Planning In Practice

When I asked Michelle Prescott of Persona People Management to tell me about her business, her clients and her services, it was quite an eye opening exercise for her. For some time she'd been providing the same HR services to the same type of clients, because they kept coming to her, or being referred to her by other consultants. She had been labeled as someone who did particular work for certain types of companies. As we went through the process, it became more apparent that the sort of work that Michelle had been doing wasn't actually what she loved doing. She'd been busy rebuilding her house for the last three years so hadn't done much in the way of promoting her business. As a result, the work that did come to her was not challenging her enough. She could see the benefit of a change of approach for her and her business and potential clients.

As I asked Michelle more about her business, we started to work out more about the sort of work she really likes doing and the sort of clients she wants to work with. Knowing the current, or starting point for the business, meant it was simple to decide where to go next. If we hadn't talked about the current state of the business, Michelle may not have realised just how much she wanted to change what she was doing and who she was doing it for.

Before you can start planning your marketing, you need to get really clear on what you offer and what makes your business different.

www.PersonaPM.co.uk

Where Do You Want To Be?

Now that you've worked through all the questions in Chapter One, you have a clear picture of where your business is. You know your starting point on the map. The next thing to do is to decide where you'd like to go, so that you can plan your route, so that you can arrive where you want to be, instead of just driving round and round in circles.

You might already have a good idea of where you want to take to your business – how many clients you want, how much money you want to earn and when you want to sell your business and sail off around the world into your retirement! A long term goal or a vision is a great thing to have. In order to reach it, you need to break down that goal into smaller more manageable ones that will allow you to get there, step by step. This section of your Marketing Plan will help you do that.

If you're not yet sure where you're going, don't worry, because this chapter will get you thinking about what you want to achieve and what you can achieve.

First we'll look at different ways of defining your goals – SMART and 'not so SMART'. There is no right or wrong way of defining your goals – it's what works for you and what will inspire you to build your business.

2

We'll then look at your short term, medium term and long term goals. It's usually best to start by creating your long term goal – the ultimate thing you'd like to achieve in your business. When you know what that is and when you'd like to reach it, you can create short and medium term goals that will get you there, step by step. If your long term goal is to sell your business for £5million in 5 years, just aiming for that won't get you there. You need to look at all the individual steps – the short and medium term goals that will get you there.

How SMART Are Your Goals?

Before you start thinking about and writing down your goals, a few words about how SMART they are. There are different ways of looking at goals and one is SMART, which many people use to set their goals.

Specific – this means you goal needs to be definite and unambiguous.

Measureable – so that you can measure the change that occurs, in terms of number of clients, size of turnover or whatever you're aiming for.

Achievable – within your reach. If you've only got two clients now and you want 100 within two months, can you really do it?

Realistic – could your business cope with taking on 98 more clients in two months? Are there that many people needing your service in your area?

Timed – when do you want to achieve your goal?

So a SMART goal for your business might be to double the number of clients over the next 12 months.

The problem with setting yourself SMART goals is that they might not inspire you. They may not encourage you to push yourself and your business, to see what you can really accomplish. Here's why:

Specific – this is not always a good thing, because it would exclude goals like those of Apple for "insanely great technology".

Measureable – so something measurably average is better than something clearly outstanding that's hard to quantify?

Achievable and Realistic – objectives you know you can achieve are much less challenging than ones you might achieve, if you really put your mind to it. The worst thing about achievable objectives is that once you meet them, you're likely to stop trying. An impossible goal like "to be the best career coach in the UK" is much more likely to inspire you. You may never get there, but every day you'll get a little closer.

Timed – this creates a dangerous illusion that you can decide not only what's going to change, but how long it will take. In reality the world is unpredictable and you need to be ready to change with it.

Some people believe that using SMART objectives assumes that the future is predictable, that it will be similar to the present and that your continual success will simply require more of what you're already doing. If you believe this, use this section of your Marketing Plan to set goals for yourself and your business that really inspire you, even if you never quite reach them.

If you'd prefer to set SMART goals, that's fine too. The framework works really well for some people, especially if you've not done much goal setting before. Use this part of your Marketing Plan to set SMART goals that will drive your business forward.

What Are Your Long Term Goals?

Whether you decide to use SMART goals or 'not so SMART' goals, it's now time to decide where you're going! Start with the end in mind, so think about where you want your business to be long term. This could be 10 years away, 5 years away or 3 years away – it's up to you. It could be about selling your business for a particular sum of money; it could be related to your turnover, number of clients or the reputation of your business. It's up to you to get creative and choose a goal that inspires you to strive for it. You can have more than one long term goal if you want.

Time frame	Your Long Term Goal(s)

What Are Your Medium Term Goals?

Now that you have your long term goal, you need to break it down into more manageable goals. For instance, if your long term goal is to sell your business in 5 years, a medium term goal might be to be working only 3 days a week in 12 months, which is part of the way to being able to sell a business that doesn't rely on you. If your goal is to be named the best in your field in the UK, a medium term goal could be to be seen as the best in your county in a year's time. You can have as many medium term goals as you like to help you reach your long term goal.

Time frame	Your Medium Term Goal(s)

What Are Your Short Term Goals?

You should be getting the hang of this process now, because it's time to break your medium term goals down into short term ones – goals that you can almost reach already. So if your medium term goal is to be working 3 days a week in 12 months time, a short term goal could be to review your current working practices to see how you can grow a business that doesn't rely on you. Another could be to look at your staff or whatever team you have, to see what needs to be done to build a solid team of people around you, who can work while you're away from the office. Linked to this, another short term goal could be to spend some time with an HR or recruitment consultant, to see what they advise in terms of growing your team.

Your short term goals can also be marketing goals. One could be to add a page to your website telling people about the sort of people you're looking for, to help you grow your team. Another could be related to finding networking groups where you can meet the people you need to advise you and help you build your team.

As with your medium term goals, you can have as many as you like. If your medium term goal is 12 months away, you might need one main short term goal for each of those 12 months.

Time frame	Your Short Term Goal(s)

 # Summary

So now you know where your business is going! The next chapter of the book will help you work out how you're going to get there.

Planning in Practice

Matthew Kane is the Chief Operating Officer at LKC, an international chemical regulatory consulting firm based in Switzerland. They work with clients all round the world and spend a lot of time building up strong relationships with their clients. The firm was created in 2001 by its CEO David, Matthew's father, whose thoughts are now turning to retiring, so he can focus on spending more time with his grandchildren and playing golf.

One of Matthew's roles is to plan the future direction of the business, as it grows and changes. He now sets the long term goals for the business, which are usually on a five year time scale. If he only focused on those long term goals, the business would struggle to meet them. This means that the long term goals are broken down into medium term goals, 2-3 years away; and short term goals, for the next 12 months.

Once a year, Matthew and I meet up to discuss LKC's Marketing Plan and to look at the company's goals. With the long term goals in mind, we plan the best marketing to be done in order to help the company achieve each of the short term goals. At each review session, we look at which of the short term goals have been achieved and how. We then plan short term goals for the next 12 month period, which allows us to ensure that the company will achieve its medium term goals.

We don't leave a review of the marketing and goals to an annual review. We discuss the marketing requirements for the short term goals on a monthly basis, to make sure that progress is kept on track.

Decide on the long term goals you want to achieve for your business. Then break them down into more manageable medium term and short term goals, so that you can plan the best marketing to help you achieve each of your goals.

www.LKC-Ltd.com

How Will You Get There?

3

Now that you know the starting point of your new marketing journey and where you're going, the next stage to plan is how you're going to get there – the strategies you're going to use.

Whatever sort of journey you're on, you need to work out the best way of getting to your destination. Will you drive or take the train? How will you get to the station, and if you drive there, where will you leave your car? There are lots of options to consider and you need to select the most appropriate, which will be based on your starting point and your destination.

You need to know the starting point of your journey (where you are now) and your destination (your goals) before you can work out which strategies are the best ones for you. This information will help you select the best strategies to use. If you're not completely clear about where you are and where you're going with your business, this is a good time to go back and review Chapters One and Two.

There are four main strategies you can consider, when deciding how to get to your destination. Unlike with an actual journey, you can use more than one of the strategies. In fact you could use all four of them in combination, if appropriate, to help you reach your goals.

Why do you need a strategy? For the very same reason that you set goals for your marketing and your business. You could just set off and try lots of different marketing activities, in the hope that they will take you to your goals – a bit like just turning up at a bus stop and hoping that one of the buses that stops there is going your way. Or you could plan the best approach and only spend your valuable time and money on what you know will work. Having a strategy and following it is much cheaper in the long run than the scatter-gun approach to marketing.

The four strategies are based on your clients – current ones and potential ones – and your products and services – existing ones and new ones you can develop. There are four ways in which you can combine these elements, giving four strategies. Each one is explained in the rest of this chapter. Work through them in the order they appear, to decide which one(s) will work best for you.

Selling Existing Services To Existing Clients

The first of the four strategies to consider is the simplest and most cost effective for many consultants and coaches. It is about selling more of your existing products and services to your existing clients.

If you provide one day of consultancy to a client each month, can you sell them more of your time and give them two days a month? If you sell coaching programmes of 10 sessions over 10 weeks to your clients, can you provide an additional 10 sessions over the next 10 weeks, to the same clients?

This strategy is the simplest and most cost effective because it involves you doing more of what you're already doing, with clients you already have. Your clients know and trust you, making them the people who are the most likely to buy more from you. Your services are already established and getting good results, so they are the easiest to promote to your clients, who already know that they work.

Selling more of your existing services to your existing clients doesn't need a huge investment in marketing or time. It's about spending time with your clients – outside the time you spend working with them – to tell them how investing in more of your time will benefit them. It's about keeping in touch with your clients on a regular basis and treating some of them to lunch now and then!

How can you sell more of your existing services to your existing clients?

....

....

....

....

Selling New Services To Existing Clients

Strategy number two is about selling some new products and services to your existing clients. These people already know and trust you – and hopefully you keep in touch with them on a regular basis. This means that you can talk to your happy clients about the sort of new products and services they'd like you to provide for them. You can create new things to sell them, based on how you're already helping them and other problems they need help with. Because they know and trust you and know that what you already do for them works, they will be open to hearing about how else you can support them.

What new products and services can you create? If your service is based around your time, think about how you can package your knowledge into products, like books, fact sheets and workshops. If you provide 10 face to face coaching sessions in a package, could you create a 'quick start' programme of 4 shorter, more intensive sessions, to help clients get started with a new project?

What new products and services can you create for your existing clients?

3

....

....

....

....

Selling Existing Services To New Clients

The third strategy you can consider looks at selling your existing services – the ones that you know work and are loved by your existing clients – to new clients with whom you've not worked before.

Your existing services have a proven track record. Hopefully you've got some great testimonials from your clients and case studies that show why clients came to you and how you helped them. These recommendations are what new clients will want to hear, before they work with you. Your existing clients know that you're really good at what you do; your potential clients need to see, hear and read the proof. This strategy is about getting some help from your current clients, to help you sell your services to some new clients.

How can you sell your existing services and products to new clients?

....

....

Selling New Services To New Clients

The final strategy is usually the hardest – and can be the most expensive to carry out successfully. While it usually involves the most risk, strategy four can also bring you the biggest returns.

Why is it so risky and expensive? Because it's about selling brand new products and services that have no track record, to potential clients who don't know you, let alone trust you. You have no proof that your new products and services can do what you say they'll do, because no one has bought them yet, or used them long enough to be able to see the results. This means that you can't rely on existing clients to tell people how great you are.

In addition, this strategy is about finding new clients, with whom you have no reputation. They've not worked with you before – they might not even have heard of you – so selling them your expertise is going to be harder and require some really targeted marketing. If you're up for a challenge and have already done everything you can or want to do with the first three strategies, then this one is for you!

Do you want to be brave and develop new products and services to sell to brand new clients?

....

....

Summary

How many strategies are you going to use to promote your business? Have you worked out which ones to use? Whichever ones you're going to use, start at the top of the list and work your way down. Strategy one is the easiest and most cost effective, while strategy four is usually the most expensive and risky – even though it can provide the biggest returns. Even if you're going to use a combination of strategies, start at the top of the list and work your way down it for the best overall results.

Chapter Four will help you identify your ideal clients – the people you really want to work with. Then in Chapter Five we'll look at combining your chosen strategies with your ideal clients, to work out the best marketing activities you can use for each strategy.

3

Planning In Practice

SR Consulting supports business owners with an impartial, insightful sounding board to help take their businesses forward. They give support to remove barriers that stifle the smooth running of businesses and help clients create realistic plans, tailored to their needs. They developed a clever tool, their Business Barometer, to assess clients' businesses and identify areas in which they need support.

When we looked at how to grow SR Consulting, we considered four different strategies they could use, based on their existing and new clients, and their current services and new ones they could create.

For most businesses, the simplest way to grow is by promoting more of their existing services to their existing clients. To use this first strategy, SR Consulting needed to create a database of clients, so they could keep in touch and remind them of the help they could provide. Then we looked at how to promote their existing services to new clients. Since most of their new work comes through networking and referrals, they need to allocate enough time to networking; keeping in contact with clients, the first strategy, will also encourage more referrals.

The third strategy for SR Consulting was promoting new services to existing clients. The Business Barometer was a great starting point, but the company needed to keep working with clients to earn an ongoing income. After taking clients through the Barometer, SR Consulting realised they could continue to work with clients by offering a range of tailored workshops. The simplest way to promote them was by showing clients, when presenting their Barometer results, how the workshops will help to solve the issues it highlighted.

The final strategy to consider is promoting brand new services to new clients. We decided that using the first three strategies would provide SR Consulting with the growth needed, without spending time and money on this last, most risky strategy.

Consider a range of marketing strategies to find the best combination for the growth you want.

www.SR-Consult.co.uk

Who Are Your Ideal Clients?

Chapter Four: Targets

When someone asks you who your clients are, is your answer something like "anyone with a pulse and a cheque book"?

If it is, I'm going to let you into a secret. No matter how hard you try, you are always going to struggle to grow your business. You might think that trying to attract every sort of client to your business is a great way of getting more clients to work with you. But that's not true. Trying to work with every different kind of business means that you will always be chasing everyone you meet, working hard to persuade them to work with you. It means that you will agree to work with clients who don't really value what you do and how much you want to charge. They will beat you down on price and then want everything done really quickly. They won't recommend you to other businesses, because they don't think you're that special.

Do you really want to work with clients like that?

If your answer is no, then read on to find out how to identify and attract your PERFECT clients.

Your perfect clients are the ones who come and find you. They want exactly what you want to offer them and they want to pay what you want to charge. They are a joy to work with and they always recommend you to other businesses. But there is a trick to finding them. Nearly every consultant or coach that starts a business begins by doing whatever comes along. The idea of sitting around waiting for people to come to you is a strange one, but it's one that you need to understand. When you know who your perfect clients are and what you want to offer them, you'll be able to attract them to you, instead of having to chase after them. You can save time by focusing your attention on only working with clients who really appreciate what you do and who pay you what you're worth. You can save money by only marketing to your perfect clients and you can make more money from working with them.

How do you find your perfect clients? It's a four stage process, but before you get into it, do you already have a perfect client? If you do, imagine you're sitting with them, talking to them, as you go through the four stages. If you don't yet have a perfect client, you can create them in your mind and design them exactly as you want them.

4

 Positive Attributes

The first thing you need to do is write a list of the attributes and positive qualities of your perfect clients. What sort of people are they? Are they looking for a quick fix or a long term relationship? Do they want a cheap solution or will they pay for quality? Are they positive, hard working and open to change or quite the opposite? Be as specific as you can, listing only positive aspects of the people you want to work with – not the businesses you want to work with.

There are no right or wrong answers to this, because your list of positive attributes will be different to everyone else's list.

Start your list here:

....

....

....

....

....

....

....

....

This list can be as long as you like and you can keep adding to it as you think of more positive qualities.

What Makes Your Perfect Clients Tick?

The next thing to do is ask your perfect client what makes them tick.

There are five questions to ask them. Use the space to write the answers you get.

What gets you out of bed in the morning?

....

....

Who is the most important person to you?

....

....

What is most important to you?

....

....

What do you want to achieve in your life?

....

....

What do you love about your life?

....

....

When you've got the answers to these questions and your list of positive attributes, look over them. What do you notice about these people? Do they remind you of anyone? Do you see yourself in the answers you've written down?

Here's the clever bit that will make your marketing easy. The Law of Attraction, when applied to business, says that people want to work with people just like them. This means that if you are hard working, passionate about helping other people and you get out of bed in the morning because you like a challenge, chances are that your perfect clients are just the same. It means that you will find it difficult to work with people who don't really care about what they do or are only in it for the money. Trying to attract people like that to do business with will be hard work and you won't enjoy the work you do for them. On the other hand, when you know what sort of people your perfect clients are, you'll find it easy to attract them – they will actually come and find you! How much fun will that be? How much time and money can you save on your marketing now?

4

What Do You Want To Offer Your Perfect Clients?

The third stage of this process is where you get to write a list of all the things that your perfect clients are allowed to expect of you. It's not a list of all the things you **think you should** provide; it's a list of things you **want** to provide.

For instance, my ideal clients can expect to always have the phone answered when they call, between 9am and 5pm Monday to Friday; outside those times they can expect to talk to an answer phone.

My ideal clients can also expect a trusted network that we will share with them, honest feedback (if we don't think a particular marketing activity will work, we'll say so and suggest an alternative) and a positive attitude. They can also expect us to deliver affordable marketing solutions that are specific to their business and that we have a genuine interest in helping them to grow their business.

Has that given you some ideas to get started?

Write your own list here:

....

....

....

....

....

....

....

*You can keep adding to this list, as you think of more things you **want** to offer your perfect clients.*

What Do You Need To Improve In Order To Be More Attractive?

The best way to attract more of your perfect clients to you is to become more attractive to them. How do you do this? By making sure that everything you want to offer your perfect clients can be delivered 100% of the time.

Look over the list of what you want to offer your clients, which you wrote on the previous page. Can you deliver every single aspect, all the time? For each thing you wrote on the list, decide if you can currently provide it 100% of the time. Put any that don't quite make it into a new list. If you think you're nearly there with some items on the first list, put them into the second list. Be critical and only leave out those elements that you can do easily, every day, even in your sleep.

Write your list of improvements here:

....

....

....

....

....

4

This new list is your list of what you need to work on, to become more attractive to your existing clients and to the potential clients who are looking for you. Look at your list every day and do one thing to improve one aspect of your business each week. If you feel that you don't give honest feedback to clients when you want to, focus on doing that for a week, in all the interactions you have with your clients and prospects. This was on my improvement list when I first went through this exercise. As soon as I started giving honest feedback to clients, I noticed how much more they trusted me and how easy it was to develop better relationships with my perfect clients. (I also noticed that those clients who didn't like receiving honest feedback weren't really perfect and they didn't stick around for long!)

Putting It Into Practice

As with any aspect of your Marketing Plan, don't tuck your list of improvements away in a drawer and forget about it. Write it out and stick it to your wall by your desk; or put it onto your computer screen so you can see it every day. Here are some tips to help you be more attractive to your perfect clients.

Let your perfect clients know how perfect they are. Invite them to lunch or coffee. If you can't meet face to face, arrange to spend at least half an hour with them on the phone. Share your list of improvements with them and let them know they are one of your perfect clients. Hearing that will strengthen your relationship with them – because it's very flattering to be told that you're perfect and ideal! Tell them you want to work with more people like them and they will help you find them.

Let go of not so perfect clients. 'Sacking' a client is something that most consultants and coaches would not dream of doing, especially in the first few years of business. You need every piece of work you can get, right? Wrong! When your perfect clients are people who value your expertise and want to pay for it, if you try to work with someone who does not value external help, they will ask for a discount. They will want the work done as quickly as possible and yet will take ages to pay – in fact you'll probably have to chase them to get paid. Why waste time doing a piece of work just for the money, when you could work with a perfect client who loves what you do and pays you in advance?

Share your expertise. Sharing advice can be very attractive, so start speaking and writing about what you do. Give presentations at networking groups and run seminars; write a newsletter and publish articles. When you start to think like the expert you are, your perfect clients will be attracted to you.

Work with your competitors. If you've got less than perfect clients that you don't want to work with anymore, you need to refer them to another supplier for whom they are perfect. Helping a not so perfect client or prospect find someone who can help them will work wonders for your reputation. Rather than just dumping them or turning them away, by finding them the perfect supplier, they will always remember how you helped them. To do this, you need to know your competitors and who their perfect clients are. Get to know them through networking and over coffee.

And finally, accept that you can't always see where things are going or how they're going to work out. Thinking about perfect clients in terms of the attributes of the people rather than the businesses that you want to work with and working on making your business more perfect, is probably a very new concept for you. It might go against everything you've heard in the past about marketing and finding new clients. Using the Law of Attraction in marketing can take some getting used to, so just go with the flow and accept that things will work out – even if you're not sure how!

When you know who your perfect clients are, you can head to Chapter Five where we'll look at working out the best marketing activities you can use to tell them about your business and attract them to you.

4

Planning In Practice

Barry Grinham runs Camp Energy, a number of fun, energy packed camps for children, during school holidays. He has over 40 years' experience in the health and fitness industry and loves helping people of all ages to become fitter and healthier.

When we started to identify Barry's ideal clients, we went through the process outlined in this chapter. Barry told me that his favourite clients – some of the parents who bring their children to his camps – were polite and approachable, that they know what they want and are open to ideas and suggestions. They are very loyal and love to recommend his camps, wanting their friend's children to have the same fun experience that their children have. They are particularly interested in the health and wellbeing of their children and are happy to pay a premium for an experience that puts a major focus on helping their children to stay fit and healthy.

Then I asked Barry what makes his clients tick. The thing that gets them out of bed in the morning is their children; they are the most important people in their lives. They want to know that their children are being well looked after, when they can't be with them.

Even though most of Barry's clients are the mothers of the children who come to his camps, he suddenly started to see the similarities between them and himself. Ask Barry who is the most important person to him, and he'll tell you it's his daughter. What is most important to him? His daughter's health and wellbeing.

When you run a service business, you'll find that your ideal clients share many of your values. When you're clear about what's important to you, it will become easier to attract ideal clients to your business.

www.CampEnergy.com

What Is The Best Marketing To Do?

Chapter Five: Tactics

As you've been working your way through the steps to creating your powerful Marketing Plan, by now you'll know exactly where your business is – the starting point for your journey – and where you are going – your objectives. You will have identified the best strategies to use to reach your goals and you'll know exactly who your ideal clients are. If you haven't completed the exercises in the previous chapters of this book, now is a good time to go back and do them. Until you know where you're going, how you're going to get there and who you're looking for, any marketing that you do will be very hit and miss. The activities you use may not be the best ones to find the people you're looking for.

There is no need to rely on 'trial and error' with your marketing. There are certain marketing tactics that work for specific targets and objectives and this chapter will help you work out which ones are the best for you. This will save you a lot of time and money! Instead of using a scatter gun approach or trying something because you think it 'might' work, you can pick the marketing activities that you know will work for your business.

So, before you carry on reading, make sure you know exactly where you are, where you're going, how you're going to get there and who your ideal clients are. If you're ready, then read on! In this chapter we'll start by helping you work out where your clients 'hang out' so that you can put your marketing messages in places that your prospective, ideal clients will see them. We will look at some of the different marketing activities that you can use, dividing them into 'online' and 'offline' activities. Then we'll look at how to integrate all your chosen marketing activities, to make sure they're all pulling in the same direction for you, to generate great results than they can do on their own.

5

Where Do Your Clients Hang Out?

Now that you know who your ideal clients are – the people that you really want to work with, who will love working with you – you need to think about where they hang out. When you know this, you can put your marketing messages in places where they will see them and respond to them. If you just splash your messages everywhere, your prospective clients will see them, but so will hundreds of other people that you don't want to work with, so most of your effort and money will be wasted. Putting your messages in places where your prospects won't see them will waste your effort and money too.

Look back at the notes you made in Chapter Four, where you identified your ideal clients. When you combine their positive attributes and what makes them tick, with the products and services that you want to provide, you'll get an even clearer picture of who these people are and where they hang out.

For example, if you provide weight loss advice to people who want to get fitter and live a healthier lifestyle, leaving a brochure in a pub won't bring you many enquiries – if any. You will have more success if you leave that same brochure in a doctor's surgery.

If you specialise in helping women become more successful and assertive at work, promoting your business in magazines aimed at men will be a waste of time.

For ideal clients over a certain age, will they see your message on the internet? More and more people are going online, regardless of their age, but you still need to know where on the internet they spend time. What other products and services are they looking for? Which websites do they visit?

Where do your clients hang out? Use the space below to write down everywhere your clients 'could' spend time – in the column on the left, put the places they do and the column on the right for places they don't.

My clients hang out here	My clients don't hang out here
e.g. Industry specific networking events	e.g. Trade exhibitions

Online Marketing

Now that you have a good idea of where your clients spend their time and where you can put messages for them to see, it's time to look at the different marketing activities you can use.

First we'll look at Online Marketing. This is anything that can be done electronically, or using the internet. These activities have been increasing massively in the last few years and more and more are becoming available all the time. If you're not careful, you could spend all your time online, trying out different marketing activities and getting involved in conversations that won't necessarily get you to where you want to go. Doing some planning before you decide where to spend your time and money will help you to save both.

Below is a non-exhaustive list of online marketing activities – you can add any others you think of. Using you knowledge of who your ideal clients are and where they hang out, write notes next to each activity about whether or not you think they would be effective for you. In Chapter Six we'll look at how to decide, from a financial point of view, which ones are best to use and in what order.

Can I use these Online Marketing tactics?

- Your website
- Other websites
- YouTube
- Videos
- Email Newsletters
- Twitter
- LinkedIn
- Facebook
- Other social media websites
- Websites of offline networking groups
- Pay Per Click Advertising
- Online PR
- Teleseminars
- Webinars
- Blogs
- Email marketing

Do you have any more to add to the list?

....

....

....

....

5

Offline Marketing

Now consider the Offline Marketing you can do. This is anything that isn't done electronically and doesn't use the internet. Some people consider this to be 'traditional' marketing; but don't ignore these tactics, thinking that they are out of date. They can all work well, when used correctly, to attract the right clients with the right message. Some Offline Marketing can work better than the Online versions, because fewer people use them and you can have a greater impact than your competitors.

As for Online Marketing use the list below to start thinking about what Offline Marketing you can do.

Can I use these Offline Marketing tactics?

- Advertising in papers and magazines
- Posters
- Networking
- Exhibitions
- Presentations
- Seminars and workshops
- Cold Calling
- Telemarketing
- CSR – Corporate Social Responsibility
- Direct Mail

- Brochures
- Fliers and leaflets
- Writing a Book
- Press releases
- Press articles
- Meetings with existing clients

You can add more ideas here:

....

....

....

....

....

....

....

....

....

....

Integrating Your Marketing

So now you're building up a picture of which marketing activities you can use to promote your business. Whatever activities you eventually decide to use, once you've been through the exercises in the next chapter, there is one thing that will make your marketing even more effective, for no further investment. It can actually save you a lot of time and all it takes is a bit of creative thinking.

The key is to integrate your chosen marketing activities, to make sure they're all pulling in the same direction for you, to generate bigger results than each of them can do on its own. Getting your message across to a prospect effectively can take a number of hits – they need to hear from you many times before they decide to buy from you. A prospect might meet you at a networking event, read a newsletter you've written, hear about you from one of your clients, read an article that's been written about you in a magazine and also visit your website. If they hear a different message from each source, they won't have a clear picture of what you do and how you can help them. They might even be confused about what you do, which could put them off ever asking for your services.

So how do you integrate your marketing? Whatever mix of activities you use, you need to put out a consistent message. This means that your website needs the same branding and logo as your business card and your blog. The style and language you use in your newsletter needs to be the same as that on your website. The way you network with prospective clients needs to be consistent with how you work with your actual clients. Any mismatch will reduce the effectiveness of your marketing.

Integrating your marketing also means using your materials across different channels, so that you don't have to keep producing new content. For example, if you write a regular newsletter, some of the copy can also be published in your blog. Snippets of the copy can be put out on Twitter and used as updates on social media websites such as Facebook and LinkedIn. The newsletter article can be published on your website and sent to online article distribution websites. The same article can be sent to the press for publication in offline magazines. You should note that it's not wise to use exactly the same material for every single channel – you might need to adapt and tailor it, according to how and where you're using it, but you get the idea of integration.

5

🍎 Summary

The number of marketing activities that you can use to promote your business is constantly on the increase. New Online tactics and platforms are being developed all the time, in an attempt to get you to part with your money. With the growth in Online Marketing, the people who sell Offline Marketing are working even harder to persuade you to spend your money with them. If you're not careful, you will find yourself being pulled in all sorts of directions, trying a little bit of something here (just to see how it works, without investing too much) and a little bit of something else over there. You will spread yourself, your budget and your message too thinly.

There is nothing wrong with using a wide range of marketing activities to promote your business. In fact, I recommend that you use up to ten different activities. This means that if one isn't working as well as it could be, or stops working all together, you've still got plenty of other activity to rely on. If you rely on just three tactics to bring in new business and one of them stops working, then you could end up losing one third of your new business! That's a huge chunk that you can't afford to lose! (If you're thinking 'this sounds rather drastic and won't happen to me', just think what would happen if your website server crashes and can't be restored for a couple of days; or if there's a postal strike just before you send out a seasonal direct mail shot.)

So you can use as many marketing activities as you like – just make sure that you plan them all carefully, to make sure that they will all work together and you'll get the great results you're looking for. In the next chapter we'll look at how much all this marketing might cost, how much you can afford and how to decide where to invest your Marketing Budget.

Planning In Practice

Options HR provides valuable HR advice to businesses that don't have their own HR department. To attract new clients and encourage existing clients to use more of their services, they use a range of both Online and Offline Marketing tactics, all integrated and working together.

The company had a brochure website that was static and not easy to update. There was no way of keeping in touch with existing clients or networking contacts. A number of clients used the HR services on an ad hoc basis when there was a problem to be sorted out; they weren't aware of all the services available.

After a planning session that showed a large potential for winning more business from existing clients, we put together a plan for a range of integrated marketing. We moved the website to a Content Management System so we could update it whenever we needed to. We started writing and publishing email newsletters, every two months, for existing clients, past clients and other contacts. This is a simple way of the company keeping in touch with everyone on a regular basis and the newsletters provide useful, up to date HR advice.

We ran quarterly HR clinics where clients and prospects could bring their HR issues to a confidential meeting and get help from the HR specialists and the other people around the table. The first two sessions attracted just a handful of visitors, but generated new work for the company. For the third event, a special email invitation was sent to all clients, inviting them to bring colleagues or their own clients to a session specifically around Performance Management. A Telesales specialist was used for a day, to call everyone on the list. Everyone who accepted was emailed a few days before the meeting to remind them. This session attracted nearly 20 people, including some prospective clients, who were all able to get help with their specific issues and pick up expert tips.

A video camera was used on the day, to capture the presenter giving advice on Performance Management. A number of short video clips have been put onto YouTube to be found by anyone who needs them and encouraging people to visit the website for more advice. There are links from the email newsletters to the videos and they have been embedded into the website for visitors to watch. All past issues of the newsletters are also available on the website, building up a valuable resource for clients and prospective clients.

By planning and then integrating a range of marketing activities, the results have dramatically increased for Options HR. Marketing works better when it works together.

www.OptionsHR.co.uk

How Much Will Your Marketing Cost?

By now, if you have been working through the chapters of this book in sequence, you will have a really good idea of the marketing that will work and bring you new clients. You will have a list of marketing activities that you want to use, which you know will attract clients to your business and keep your existing clients coming back for more.

There is one very important thing that you need to consider carefully, before you go any further. How much is all this marketing going to cost you and how much can you afford? While it would be great if you have enough money to carry out all the marketing that you want to do, you probably do not have a limitless budget to spend. You need to invest in your marketing, to make sure that your business grows; and at the same time you need make sure you have enough to live on, without blowing it all on your marketing.

Many business owners fail because they do not plan their marketing properly and because they do not consider the finances. They start a business with a great idea and loads of enthusiasm, but they just do not have the financial backing to succeed. You do not have to have a huge budget to make a go of your business and your marketing, but you need to know how much you can afford and how best to spend it, before you get your cheque book out.

Do you need a budget, or should you just make it up as you go along? The answer to that question is that you should definitely start out with a budget. Even if you do not stick to it, you need one to start with. The reason for this is because it will stop you spending far more than you can afford. When someone comes along with a 'great offer' you will know whether or not you can really afford it and what return you might get from your investment.

Do you need money to start up and run a successful coaching, consulting or training business? Many people try it without any financial backing and they usually struggle. They do things on the cheap and it shows. If you are looking to develop a professional business, you need a certain amount of money behind you, to be able to do a proper job and to develop a business that will thrive.

This chapter starts by helping you decide on your budget and what you can afford to invest. Then we will look at what different types of marketing might cost, and how to work out the possible return on investment you will get from them. The final section of the chapter is a bonus because it lists some of the marketing you can do for free, along with some thoughts on how you can use them and what to watch out for.

6

🍎 What Can You Afford?

How do you decide on your budget? There are a number of methods you can use, outlined below. Use the right hand column for your notes about each one and the possible size of your budget.

	Budgeting Method	Your Notes
The "10%" Method	This is where you allocate 10% of your turnover to your marketing. As your business grows, so can the marketing that you can afford to do. If you are starting from the very beginning, with no clients and no turnover, you need to think about how much you can afford to get you started and find your first clients.	
The "How much have I got?" Method	This method is about looking at what funds you realistically have available to you, which you can allocate to marketing. If you have been made redundant, you might have a sum of money you can put to developing your business. If you are working while setting up your business, you can allocate a proportion of your salary. If you are already running your business, look at what money is coming in and what you can afford to invest in your marketing.	
The "How much does it cost?" Method	With this method, you need to look at all the marketing activities you identified in Chapter Five and calculate how much it will all cost. Then you need to look for that investment – either from your own savings or from external sources. You can speak to banks, investors or family to raise the funding you need. While this method might see you relying on outside help, it means you can definitely afford to do everything in a very professional manner.	

Spend some time thinking about the different ways of setting your budget and how much you can or want to spend on your marketing.

How Much Does It All Cost?

Different marketing activities all cost different amounts; and suppliers will charge you varying amounts – which is why you need a budget. When you know that you have £1000 to spend on a website, you can look for a website developer who can provide what you need for that sum. If you can afford to spend £10,000 on a website, you need to look for a very different type of website developer.

The next thing to do is take your list of marketing activities, which you created in Chapter Five, and do some research to get a feel for how much it could all cost you. If you have set your budget to a certain amount – using either of the first two methods discussed in Section One of this chapter – then you have parameters in which to work. For example, if you know that you have £5000 to spend over the next 12 months and that you need a new website, a monthly newsletter, more business cards and to attend one networking lunch every month, you can start to allocate the funds you have to the different activities. If you are using the "How much does it cost?" method for setting your budget, get out there and find out how much it all costs!

So how much does marketing cost? How long is your piece of string?! There are so many suppliers that you can speak to, with prices varying from virtually nothing to astronomical, that you need to start getting an idea of the range available. When you are looking to invest in a marketing activity, do not jump at the first opportunity. You can shop around to get exactly what you are looking for. Using the list you put together in Chapter Five, start to get a feel for the range of prices you might pay for what you need. This will help you decide where to spend your budget; it will also help you decide who to work with because you can compare prices between suppliers.

6

Marketing Acivity	Budget Price	Top of the Range

What Return Will You Get From Your Investment?

When you are working out which marketing activities you can afford to carry out, you might want to work out what return on investment (ROI) you are likely to get from each one. This can help you decide which will be the most effective, or which you should do first.

It is worth noting here that the numbers you get will not be absolute, especially if you do your marketing properly and integrate everything that you do. If you just do one marketing activity, you will be able to work exactly what the return will be, because that one thing will generate all your new business. However, if you do more than one thing – for instance if you have a website, go networking, publish a newsletter and post a blog – then potential clients will have numerous ways of hearing your marketing message. They will read about you, meet you and hear about you from a variety of sources. This means that when you ask your new clients how they heard about you, they may not actually be able to remember. If you get your marketing right, they will have heard about you from a number of sources that all reinforced your message.

ROI is a measure of the profit you earn from each investment. It's usually a percentage and in simple terms, the calculation is:

$$\frac{\text{Return} - \text{Investment}}{\text{Investment}} \times 100$$

For marketing ROI you need to think about what makes up your return and your true investment. Are you looking at the total revenue generated by a marketing activity; the gross profit, which is revenue minus the cost of goods to deliver your service; or net profit, which is gross profit minus expenses?

On the investment side, you need to think about what to include. As well as your time, you might have creative costs, printing costs, technical costs and so on.

A basic formula uses the gross profit for units sold in a particular campaign and the marketing investment for the campaign:

$$\frac{\text{Gross Profit} - \text{Marketing Investment}}{\text{Marketing Investment}}$$

ROI calculations for marketing campaigns can be complex — you may have many variables on both the profit side and the investment (cost) side. Understanding the formula is useful because it will help you produce the best possible results from your marketing budget – whatever size it is. Use these calculations to work out which of the marketing activities you've identified already in this book will give you a good return.

Chapter Nine of this book looks in detail at how you can measure your marketing. Once you have started marketing your business, you can look back at the activities you have used and work out what has worked and therefore what you should do more of. You can compare your measurements with the Return on Investment calculations you do in this section.

Free Marketing

How much marketing can you do for free? There is a great deal that you can do for free, which is ideal when you are starting out. Here are some ideas for you.

Networking – some networking events don't charge entry. You might just have to buy yourself a cup of coffee, or put up with a sponsoring organization making a presentation. The other thing to be aware of at free networking events is that they are often frequented by business people who do not want to spend much money – on their marketing or anything else, which you might like to sell to them.

Social Media – Twitter, LinkedIn and Facebook are just some of the free online tools that you can use to promote your business. There are additional paid-for upgrades, but for the most part, you can use them for free to build your online network and reputation.

Wordpress Websites – there are a growing number of website platforms, including Wordpress, which you can use for free. You might need a few design skills to make it stand apart from the hundreds of other sites that people have set up for free, but you do not need a degree in computer science to create an online presence. You can also use systems like Wordpress for publishing a regular blog and sharing your thoughts and ideas with the world.

Public Speaking – if you are comfortable standing up in front of an audience, then giving presentations at networking events is a great free marketing tool. If you have never done public speaking before, get some training before you have a go, because doing a bad job can be bad for your reputation.

Email Newsletters – these are a great way of keeping in touch with people you meet. They also allow you to explain what you do over time, educating your audience. This can take time for coaches, consultants and trainers, especially if you do a lot of different things. There are many online email newsletter systems you can use to publish a newsletter, for no cost. If your list is small, you can send out monthly newsletters without being charged. You only start paying when your list reaches a certain size.

Email Signatures – when you email anyone, be they client, supplier or prospect, you can send them marketing messages in your email signatures. As well as containing your contact details, which are essential, you can add details of new products and services, of forthcoming events, or special offers you are promoting. You can change your signature on a regular basis or have a range that you use, depending on who you are contacting.

Please don't rely on free marketing for ever, because it will only get you so far. Sooner or later you'll need to invest in your marketing and show that you're running a serious business. Free business cards will always look free and won't create the professional image you really need.

6

Summary

There is more to running a successful business than just coming up with a great idea. Once you have done some planning about what you are going to provide, to whom and how, you really need to consider the financial aspect of your idea. It is at this stage in the planning process that many people turn back, realizing that they just cannot afford to do what they want to do. For others it is the point at which they will fail, because they do not plan how much they can afford to spend. As a result, they end up spending far more than they can afford, on marketing activities that will not generate the right number and type of new clients they need for their business.

Take all the time you need to go back through this chapter and review your plan so far. Do you have a realistic list of marketing activities? Will they give you a good return on your investment? Can you afford to carry them out? Can you raise the finance you need? Before you actually start spending your hard earned finances on what you would like to do, be ruthless and realistic. Do your financial planning before you move onto Chapter Seven, where we will look at who will be doing your marketing.

Planning In Practice

When you work for a charity, every penny that you spend has to be accounted for. Every pound that is raised by supporters, donations or legacies is needed to both run the charity – to carry out the good work that it does – and to promote it, in order to raise more funds. This means that marketing budgets can be tight and charities need to look for creative ways to promote themselves.

The Oxfordshire Animal Sanctuary was set up in the 1960s and now finds new homes for cats, dogs, rabbits and guinea pigs. There are plans to develop the Sanctuary, building new kennels for the animals that stay there, while waiting for new homes. The day to day cost of running the Sanctuary and caring for all the animals is also considerable and there have been times when it has struggled to stay open.

When I asked the marketing team at the Sanctuary if they would like some free help to develop a Marketing Strategy, they jumped at the chance. While the charity is run as a proper business, when it came to looking at the cost of different marketing activities that they could carry out, we had to think very carefully about the available budget. Printing and posting a newsletter to hundreds of supporters really eats into their limited budget, so we decided to focus on building up the email list of supporters. Sending a regular email newsletter dramatically reduces the cost of keeping in touch with people every month. Since I also write the newsletter for free, they don't even need to pay a writer to create the content for them each month.

Social media will also play an increasingly important role in promoting the Sanctuary. Other than the time needed to write updates and post them, there is no cost to using platforms such as Facebook and Twitter, which work very well for the Sanctuary. Since they are also free to use, we decided to make more of YouTube, Pinterest and Instagram too.

When you're planning your marketing, think carefully about what you can afford and which marketing activities will give you the best return on your budget.

www.OxfordshireAnimalSanctuary.org.uk

6

Who Will Do It?

7

When I started planning my new business, back in 2000, I sought as much advice as I could, on how to set up and run a business. One of the best pieces of advice I received has stayed with me ever since and I frequently share it with other people who are setting up or running their own businesses, so I want to share it with you now.

I was told that, aside from what you actually do in your business – whether that is coaching, consulting, training or something else – you also have to be able to do three other things. They are admin, marketing and finance; and I was told that if you cannot do any of those three really well, you should seek help to get them done. When I started my business, I could handle the admin because there was not much to do; as I got busier I found other people, in the form of a virtual PA and a phone reception service, to help with the admin. The accounts I managed for a short time, but numbers are not my strong point, so as soon as I found myself struggling with my first tax return, I sought out a bookkeeper. I had wasted an afternoon achieving nothing, when I could have been out looking for new business. From then on I paid someone else to do what I could not do, in less than half the time.

Of the three activities – admin, finance and marketing – the last area is the one that I kept hold of from the start and that I will always do for my business. I am, after all, a Marketing Consultant, so I should know what I am doing! However, even I have my limitations. While I can happily write over 1000 words of a book in an hour (yes really!) I cannot spot the spelling errors or grammatical mistakes that a spell checker will not see. I can stand up in front of a room of 100 people, or more, and give a presentation, but I am hopeless at making cold calls and setting up appointments with people who do not know me.

When you run your own business, if you try to do everything, two things will happen. Firstly, you will spend a lot more time doing things like marketing, finance and admin than someone who is a specialist in that area. It comes naturally to them – in the same way as doing what you do to earn your fees comes naturally to you – so they can do it much more quickly than you can. Then, because you are spending so much time doing what someone else can do, you will find that you do not have time to promote your business properly or look after the clients you have.

This chapter is about looking realistically at what marketing you can do – with the time and skills that you have – and then looking at where you can find the people who can support you. It will then encourage you to think about exactly who can help you with the different marketing activities that you identified in Chapter Five, so that you can build a great team around you.

What Can You Do?

Unless you are a Marketing Consultant of some sort, you will need to look for help with some or all of your marketing. You might not be able to afford to take on a full time marketing department if you are just setting up your business, but you do need to look carefully at your marketing and decide which elements of it you can realistically handle.

To help you decide which marketing activities you can carry out, answer these questions:

	Yes	No
Are you an introvert – a shy and retiring flower?		
Or are you an extrovert – outgoing and bubbly?		
Do you enjoy writing? If so, are you any good at it?		
Are you self motivated and able to handle knock backs again and again?		
Do you enjoy talking or are you happier to listen?		
Have you ever given a speech at a wedding or similar event?		
Can you walk into a party and start talking to the first person you meet, even if you don't know them?		
Do you hate being bothered by cold callers trying to sell you something over the phone?		
Did you take Art at school and get a good grade in the exam?		
Are you a computer whizz who has been designing websites for friends since before you left school?		

There are no right or wrong answers to these questions. They are designed to get you thinking about what you are good at and what you enjoy doing. For example, if you love meeting new people and talking to strangers, then if networking is on your list of marketing activities to be carried out, you will do a great job at it and will not need someone else to go to meetings for you.

On the other hand, if you are always rude to cold callers when they phone you and you find it hard to get up when you get knocked down, if telesales is on your list of relevant marketing tools, you should find someone else do it for you.

Unless you know how to set up a website or you got a grade A at art, think about finding some help with graphic design and creating your website.

Look at the marketing activities you listed in Chapter Five and think honestly about which you can do and where you need help.

7

Top Tip

There will always be someone who knows someone who can help you for little or no money. They know the son of a friend's neighbour who builds websites for his mates at school. While he will not charge you much, will he still be on hand in a couple of years, when there is problem with your website?

Someone else in the pub will have an opinion on the best way of doing something. Unless they earn a living from doing whatever they are talking about, take their advice with a pinch of salt.

Where To Find Help

Here are just a few of the places that you can look for the people and businesses that can help you with your marketing.

The Internet – any help that you are looking for can be found by searching the internet. You can use it to search for very specific suppliers, for companies in particular areas of the country, or for specialists in certain fields. You can check out the websites of potential suppliers to get a feel for what they do and whether or not you might like working with them, before you get in touch with them.

Social media is a useful tool for finding help. If you are already using Twitter, for example, you can put the word out that you are looking for help in a particular area. People who follow you will spread the word, which will bring you recommendations and direct contact from interested suppliers.

Directories – many of these now exist online and they can be good places to compare, for example, all the telesales companies in a particular area. Do be aware that many directories take paid for entries, so just because a company is listed, it is not a guarantee that they are the best choice.

Networking – many people go to networking meetings thinking that they are just about finding new clients. In actual fact, networking meetings are a great way of meeting potential suppliers. You can start to get to know them in a more relaxed and informal situation than if individual suppliers are coming to see you. It can also save you a lot of time – instead of having a one hour meeting with three possible suppliers you can carry out your initial selection process while also doing some networking.

Networking meetings are also the ideal place to ask for recommendations. If you are looking for a copywriter to create the words for your website, ask around for recommendations. This way you can be introduced to potential suppliers without first meeting them face to face.

Clients and Colleagues – ask other business people you know for recommendations. If you see something you like – a website or brochure, for example – ask who produced it.

These are just a few of the places where you can find help. Start thinking about what you need and you will come with other ways of finding them.

Who Else Can Help You?

Now that you know where you need some help, it is time to look for it. At this stage, you may not be able to afford to pay someone else to do everything on this list, but it is still worth looking for help because you might not have to pay for it. Think of how you might be able to help them, in return for their services.

Use the space below to recreate the list of marketing activities you identified in Chapter Five – both online and offline marketing. Next to each one, start filling in the names of people or companies you already know who can help you.

7

Marketing Acivity	Who Can Help?	Who Else Do I Need To Talk To?

Depending on how many marketing activities you are going to use, this table might not be big enough and you might need another sheet of paper or a spreadsheet! Use the table to start filling in the gaps by searching for the support you need.

Summary

Many people who start up their own businesses think they have to do everything themselves. Hopefully this chapter has shown you the value of getting some help with your marketing and building a team around you. Take your time to build this team, looking for the right people to work with. You will meet people who have the right skills to help you, but are they the right people for you to work with? You need people who will help you create the right impression to your clients and who understand what you want to achieve. You need to get on with the people you are working with; otherwise you will find yourself constantly struggling to explain your ideas and aspirations to them. They need to 'get' you and your business.

Now it is time to go on to Chapter Eight which help you schedule all your marketing activities, to make sure they get done – whether you are doing them yourself or someone else is doing them for you.

Planning In Practice

Many owners of growing businesses think that they have to do their own marketing, as well as everything else that needs to be done within their business. They try to cut costs by doing their own marketing, admin and finances. Too often, this leads to ineffective marketing and not enough time to do the work that actually brings in the money.

Luckily, this is not something that Amanda Downs at Sales Growth Expert has tried to do. Amanda's business helps other people to become sales growth experts, by giving them the support, mentoring and training they need, to be become highly effective sales people. She recognised that she needed to build a team around her, to carry out a range of marketing activities. When we started working together, she had already found a talented website designer to create a new website for her. However, writing marketing content is not something that Amanda wanted to do. It's not one of her core skills, so I created the new content for her website, so she could give the right marketing message to prospective clients.

Something that Amanda did want to write was an ebook, in which she could share her knowledge and expertise. Because writing is not a core skill for her, she asked me to edit the book, to make sure that it was highly professional and gave out the right message. While I can edit content, I'm not a graphic designer, so someone else was brought in to work on the look of the book, so that it gave the right visual message. One way in which we decided to promote the ebook was through an email campaign. I love writing newsletters and blogs – which I also do for Amanda – but I don't enjoy writing short sales copy. For this, we brought in a different copywriter who had the right skills for the job.

Regardless of the number people in your business, look at who has the marketing skills that you need. If you don't have the best skills in-house, build a team around you, who can help carry out the marketing you need.

www.SalesGrowthExpert.co.uk

Chapter Eight: Minutes

Marketing and growing your business is a journey. It's not something that's going to happen overnight and there are no short cuts or short term fixes. It takes time to build up a reputation, especially if you're starting a new business. Just because you've opened your doors, that doesn't mean that people will suddenly queue up to do business with you. Just because you do a bit of marketing – send out a newsletter or launch your website – that won't necessarily make the phone start ringing right away. Even if you've been in business for a while, you can't expect a new marketing initiative to kick in overnight; and the same applies if you're promoting a brand new product or service.

Effective marketing is about doing the planning, to make sure that the right activities get done at the right time. It's about being prepared so that you get your press release out in plenty of time to promote the event you're running in three months time. It's about making sure that the right amount of marketing gets done, on a regular basis, to keep filling your pipeline of prospects, to bring you a steady stream of new clients and business. Many coaches and consultants get stuck on a 'feast and famine' rollercoaster, where you do lots of marketing and bring in plenty of work, that keeps you so busy that you don't have time to do any marketing. Suddenly the work dries up and so you start doing lots of marketing again. The work floods in and you're back to the point where you don't have time to any marketing. Effective, planned marketing will help you get off that rollercoaster – and help you stay off it.

This chapter explains why ad hoc marketing does not work and how you need to take account of this when you plan your marketing. We will look at the importance of knowing how long different marketing activities take to set up and produce results; and show you a way of planning all your marketing activities, so that you know what to do and when to do it.

8

Ad Hoc Marketing Does Not Work

"I've tried direct marketing and it doesn't work."

"I went networking once but it didn't bring me any new clients."

These are phrases that I hear on a regular basis. It's a bit like saying "I had one ice skating lesson and still didn't win the first competition I entered." Instead of falling over and hurting yourself, you need to invest in a number of lessons and do plenty of practice, to make sure that you reach the right standard. Sending one piece of direct mail without researching it first and doing any follow up afterwards is unlikely to get you any results. In the same way, going to one networking meeting isn't enough time to allow new people to get to know you properly. When you provide a service such as coaching or consulting, your prospective clients need to trust you before they will share their problems with you and part with their money. You need to build up a relationship with them.

When I first started helping coaches and consultants with their marketing, it was commonly thought that it took up to six 'touches' with a prospect before they would buy from you. This meant that a prospective client might, for example, meet you at a networking meeting (1), they might read about you in a press article (2), read an issue of your newsletter (3), hear you speak at a presentation (4), be recommended to you by one of your clients (5) and visit your website (6). With

the development of social media, this number can be reported to be as high as 40 touches! Whatever the number, what it means is that you need to keep doing your marketing on a regular basis, using the right mix of activities, so that you 'touch' your prospects as many times as is needed, to build up the right level of trust, before they will buy from you.

When you've decided how many marketing activities you're going to use to promote your business, you need to look at how many times you need to do each one and over what period of time. It's about doing the right number of the right number of things. You can't choose 10 activities and only do each one once.

Planning your marketing also means that when someone comes along with a great offer, for a one off activity – such as an advert in a magazine or a stand at an exhibition – you'll know whether or not it's worth you doing it. If you know that advertising in certain publications works, go for it. If you know that you don't have an exhibition stand and you're not comfortable standing around handing out leaflets, you'll find it easy to turn it down.

Take the time now to go back to Chapter Five and look at the list of online and offline marketing activities that you wrote down. Are any of these ad hoc or can they all be done on a regular, sustained basis? Refine your list of activities, if you need to.

 ## Set Up Time

When you're planning your marketing, you need to think about how long different activities will take to get set up and how long it might take before you start seeing results. You need to do some research before you launch into any new venture. You also need to remember that things always take longer than you expect them to!

Use the table below to list the activities you listed in Chapter Five (making sure you remove any ad hoc activities.) Then start doing some research to find out how long each of them might take to set up. You may need to speak to a number of experts to get an idea of timings. For instance, if you're looking to create a new website, talk to some website developers about how long it might take. If you're going to run a PR campaign, speak to someone who knows how much time you need to plan the process, including lead times for magazines and papers.

Marketing Activity	Set Up Time Needed

Keep working on this table and referring back to it as you plan your marketing and work through different activities.

Scheduling Your Marketing

Once you have an idea of how long different aspects of your marketing may take and you are sure which ongoing marketing activities you are going to carry out, you need to schedule them. This means working out what will be done, on a weekly and monthly basis, to make sure that you fit some marketing into each week and month. Without a schedule, it is very easy to forget about your marketing, particularly if you are busy looking after your clients. However, if you do not find time for your marketing, you will find yourself back on the feast and famine rollercoaster before you know it.

A simple and effective way of scheduling your marketing is by using a Gantt Chart. On the next page is an example of one that might be used by a coach or consultant, over a three month period.

This Gantt Chart is just an example of what could be done. Using the chart on the next page as a guide, create your own chart to start scheduling your own marketing over the next six months.

As well as using the chart to schedule your marketing and making sure you find time to fit it in, the chart can be used to measure your marketing. If you plan to have a meeting with one client every week, you can review your chart at the end of each week to make sure you have achieved what you set out to do. If you have not hit your targets, you know you have some catching up to do in the following week. Keeping a regular eye on your marketing will really help you keep doing it, on a regular basis. Once you have made a start on your Gantt Chart, move on to Chapter Nine, which looks in more depth at how to measure your marketing, to make it even more effective.

Activity	Month 1				Month 2				Month 3			
	Week 1	Week 2	Week 3	Week 4	Week 1	Week 2	Week 3	Week 4	Week 1	Week 2	Week 3	Week 4
Newsletter		Write	Publish			Write	Publish			Write	Publish	
Blog	1 post	1 post	1 post	1 post	1 post	1 post	1 post	1 post	1 post	1 post	1 post	1 post
Twitter	20 per week	20 per week	20 per week	20 per week	20 per week	20 per week	20 per week	20 per week	20 per week	20 per week	20 per week	20 per week
LinkedIn	Update profile	Answer questions	Start discussion	Look for new connections	Update profile	Answer questions	Start discussion	Look for new connections	Update profile	Answer questions	Start discussion	Look for new connections
Networking	Bimonthly lunch	Monthly lunch		Monthly breakfast		Monthly lunch		Monthly breakfast	Bimonthly lunch	Monthly lunch		Monthly breakfast
Website update		Add factsheet to site		SEO and keyword for pages		Add book pre-launch order form to website		SEO and keyword for pages		Add factsheet to site		SEO and keyword for pages
Speaking engagements			Chamber lunch		Seminar						Networking breakfast	
Client meetings	1 per week	1 per week	1 per week	1 per week	1 per week	1 per week	1 per week	1 per week	1 per week	1 per week	1 per week	1 per week
Book	Plan content of book		Write chapters 1-3		Talk to typesetter and designer	Write chapter 4-6	Look at printing options		Find copy editor	Write chapter 7-9		
Video	Record new tips		Post on YouTube, website and newsletter		Record new tips		Post on YouTube, website and newsletter		Record new tips		Post on YouTube, website and newsletter	

8

🍎 Summary

Ad hoc marketing just does not work. Using individual activities that aren't related to anything else you are doing, or that you just do once, will end up costing you money and not attracting many new clients to your business. Whatever marketing you do, make sure you stick with it for long enough to see if it really works or not. If it does, do more of it; if not, stop doing it!

Marketing is not a quick fix that will bring you new clients over night. It takes time to set up and to get right, so make sure you allow for that time. When you schedule your marketing and plan out what you'll be doing, when and for how long, it will be much more effective. Using the Gantt Chart on page 63 as a guide, create a spreadsheet – on your computer or a large sheet of paper – where you can start scheduling your marketing keep updating it.

Planning In Practice

Research Insight is a consultancy that helps clients carry out marketing research projects, providing them with the information they need to make important business decisions. Many years ago we set up a new website for the company, which brought in a number of new clients, but very little was done to the site over time. The company is listed with a number of associations and the MD went to very occasional networking meetings.

In order to grow the business and bring in more new business, a number of ongoing marketing activities were started. Every two months an email newsletter was published to a list of contacts. It contained useful advice on using research and visitors to the website are encouraged to subscribe. As it was published, each newsletter was added to the website, thereby updating the site on a regular basis.

Every few months, a number of short videos were recorded, with the MD talking about topics similar to those in the newsletters. Once a month, a video was posted on YouTube and links were set up from the bi-monthly newsletter to the relevant video, to drive more traffic to the website. Links to the videos were also put onto the Resources section of the website – another way to update the site. When a newsletter was published it included a link to a relevant article that was posted on LinkedIn. This allowed the newsletter readers to comment on the article; it also widened the company's reach, as the article could be commented on by anyone on LinkedIn. Every two weeks, a summary of comments to be looked at on LinkedIn were sent to the MD, for him to work on.

Every three months we met with the MD of Research Insight, to discuss marketing progress and plan what should be done next. We look at what is working and do more of it; activities that are not performing properly are modified to get more from them, or stopped altogether. Everything we do is planned and fits into a schedule, so that we know what is happening, when and who is doing it. In this way, the marketing keeps getting done, allowing the MD to focus on looking after his clients and carrying out their research projects.

www.Research-Insight.com

Chapter Nine: Measurements

So you've carefully planned your marketing – you know exactly who your ideal clients are and how to attract them. You've worked out what you can afford to do, who will do it and when. Your marketing is going really well and new business is coming in. But how much of your marketing is effective? Which activities are working best? Are some performing better than others and bringing you more of the right sort of clients?

A huge number of businesses don't actively measure their marketing. They put all their time and effort in planning and carrying out their marketing and that's as far as they go. Then, a year down the line, they realise that they haven't got as much new business as they had hoped for, or they have spent more money than they had planned to, just to get enough new clients.

Successful businesses measure their marketing activity. They know what is working, what is not working and how much it is costing them. They are able to adjust their marketing as they go along, to get even greater benefits. They understand the importance of measuring their marketing.

In this chapter we'll look at what you should be measuring, to see how effective your marketing is. We'll explore the importance of reviewing your marketing to make sure you do more of what works. Then we'll expose some of the secrets of great marketing in the final section of this chapter!

9

What Do You Measure?

So what should you measure? The answer is everything! Any marketing that you do – that you decide to do as part of your Marketing Plan – needs to be measured.

You can start by measuring the number of enquiries that you generate from each activity and how much it costs for each enquiry. Go a stage further and measure the number of new clients generated from those enquiries. Some activities may generate many enquiries, but if they're not the right sort of enquiries – not your ideal clients – you will not get the conversion to clients that you want.

When you are measuring the cost, take everything into account. If you attend a regular networking meeting, include the annual fee and cost of each meeting. You can even include the time that you spend at each meeting and your time to travel there – this will show you if it's worth you driving for two hours to that networking meeting, even if it's free to attend.

Be really specific with your measurements. For example, for networking meetings, measure the effectiveness of each group you attend, as this will show you if some are better for you than others. If you advertise in newspapers or magazines, measure the results you get from each one.

Use the table below to start measuring your marketing.

Activity	Cost	Number of Enquiries	Cost per Enquiry	Number of New Clients	Cost per Client

If you need more space, create a table like this in a spreadsheet, so that you can add all your marketing activities.

Magnetic Marketing

Measure And Review

Once you've filled in the table in the previous section, have a look at it. Are there any surprises? Do you have some activities working better than others? Are others not working as well as you thought?

To use your marketing successfully, you need to be ruthless and stick to the activities that work really well for you. However, don't make any hasty decisions just yet. You need to measure your marketing on a regular basis. It's worth updating the form in Section One of this chapter once a month and comparing the figures to the previous month. Once you have results from two or three months, you'll be able to see trends. Set up a spreadsheet on your computer with a monthly reminder and it will be easier to do.

Why wait for so long before changing your marketing? Because ad hoc marketing does not work and new marketing doesn't start working overnight. If you send out press releases, you need to do it over a period of time before you start to see any results. Editors may need to hear from you a number of times before they decide to write about you; they may wait for a relevant story to suit a supplement. Their readers need to see your name a number of times before they pick up the phone.

When you provide a service such as coaching or consulting, prospective clients need to get to know you and trust you before they will work with you. Going to one networking meeting and telling the audience in just one minute what you do,

won't allow you to build the strong, trusting relationships that are needed. You need to attend a number of meetings over time, getting to know the other people there and giving them time to get to know you.

Once you have data from two or three months, look at it again very carefully. What's working? What's not working? For the activities that are working, how can you capitalise on them and do more of what works? For those that aren't working, you need to look at why. Are you saying the right things in your newsletter, blogs or tweets? Are you giving the right sort of advice and information, that your ideal clients are looking for, or are you attracting not quite ideal clients by what you're saying? Are you getting your message across at networking meetings, or is what you say just confusing people? Take all this into consideration before you make any changes – don't stop going networking all together, just because it doesn't 'seem' to be working. Focus on the groups that do work and look at why; think about refining your marketing message and trying something different, before you give up entirely!

When you do decide to stop using one particular marketing activity, you can divert the time and money you were spending on it, into one of the activities that is working, which will make it work even better. Then keep measuring and keep reviewing, as you go along, and watch what happens to your results.

9

Secrets Of Great Marketing

There are a number of secrets to great marketing. You don't need to spend lots of time and money trying to work out what's best for your business, because other people have already done the trial and error. You can learn from them and save your business a fortune.

This book has shared a number of secrets with you already, such as **ad hoc marketing doesn't work**. The fact that you are reading this book means you probably know this already, and it's worth repeating. Ad hoc marketing is where you pay for one advert in a special magazine supplement, because the salesman told you the magazine will be sent to thousands of your target clients. But it's going to people who haven't asked to receive it and who won't actively use the supplement to search for your services. They might not even know that they need your services and solutions. The salesman also told you that he could give you a great price for last minute space, so you paid it without checking your marketing budget, or making sure that the magazine would be read by your ideal clients – the people who **really** want to work with you.

But you won't do that now because you've created a Marketing Plan! The next time a salesman makes a 'great offer' you can make an informed decision about where to spend your money.

Another big secret of great marketing is that you need to **do more of what works and less of what doesn't work.** This means that you have to measure all your marketing activities, as we've seen in this chapter. If you keep plugging away at a particular marketing tactic, even though it's not working – not bringing you the enquiries or new clients that you want – then you should stop doing it. If you've run the same advert in the paper for three months and it hasn't done what the salesman promised, then either stop doing it, or change the advert – the wording, the size and/or the position. When you've been going to a particular networking meeting for six months and you've not met any of your ideal clients (and the people who you have met don't know any of them either) then it's time to stop going and to try out a different group, or a different message.

Even though you're creating a powerful Marketing Plan, remember that you can and should change it. Your plan needs to be reviewed on a regular basis – not stuck on a shelf and ignored. Look at it every week and every month to see how you're doing and how well you're meeting your targets. If you're missing the mark, make some changes to your marketing.

 ## Summary

When I ask coaches and consultants where their new business comes from, I am always amazed by the number who don't know. If you have a limitless budget to spend on your marketing, then don't waste your time measuring what works and what doesn't. Just do whatever marketing you fancy. However, if you're like most business owners and you only have a certain amount of money to spend on your marketing, you want to know that what you're spending is working hard for you. The way to do this is to measure every aspect of your marketing, on a regular and ongoing basis.

9

Hilary Backwell runs Time2Time HR, a consultancy that helps business with their HR issues. She sorts out many different people problems and helps to prevents issues from arising in the first place. Hilary really gets to know her clients and provides a very personal level of service. Because her clients need to get to know her and trust her, networking is a very effective marketing tool for her business. At networking meetings, her prospective clients can meet her face to face, find out what she's like and build up the right level of trust they need, before they'll share their people problems.

There are many different networking events that Hilary can attend on a weekly and monthly basis. Once she had been working with me for about a year, and trying out many of the different networking groups, we sat down and looked at the results she'd achieved from each of the different groups. She had been recording the number of meetings she attended and the source of all her clients. There were a couple of groups that consistently introduced Hilary to new clients; there was one event at which Hilary could spend time with people who regularly recommended her to clients.

However, there was one group that was not working. Hilary is a keen golfer and joined a networking group that allowed her to play golf and network at the same time. It should have been the perfect way for Hilary to meet potential clients who share her passion for golfing. When we looked at the numbers, it became obvious that this was not happening. Hilary felt that she was spending far too much time at each golfing event and was not meeting the right sort of people. So she took the sensible decision not to renew her membership of that group. The result is that Hilary now has more time to look after the growing list of clients she is meeting from the networking groups that do work.

Measure your marketing on a monthly basis to make sure that you only do the marketing that actually works for your business.

www.Time2TimeHR.com

Why is this book called Magnetic Marketing? Because when marketing is done properly, it can help bring clients to your business. They will phone you and ask to work with you; they will turn up at your door and beg you to take them on!

In the past, marketing was about persuading people to work with you. You had to spend time chasing after prospects who you thought needed your services. You had to spend a lot of time explaining your services to them and how they couldn't live without them.

Marketing has changed and it's now much easier to grow the business you want to run, with the sort of clients you really want to work with. When you know where you are at the start of your marketing journey you can plan exactly where you want to go and how you're going to get there. Instead of driving round in circles, you can take a direct route to your future. Instead of taking the scatter-gun approach to marketing and working with anyone who will pay you, if you're selective about your clients, they will find it easier to find you. By focusing on what they want from you, you can make your business far more attractive to exactly the right sort of clients who will really value you and help your business to grow.

When you know who you're looking to attract, you can plan the marketing that will get the right message to the right places for your ideal clients to see, hear and read. Some planning around what you can afford, what help you need and how long it might all take will only help to make your marketing far more effective, giving you an edge over your competitors, who are still rushing around trying to attract everyone. Then you perfect your marketing by measuring everything you do and focussing more on what works best. The result is a successful business that will be able to grow and develop the reputation you want.

If you work through all the sections in this book and spend time on the exercises, you'll be able to create a Marketing Plan that will help you become magnetic to your clients. Keep reviewing and refining your Plan on a regular basis and those clients will keep beating a path to your door. Before you know it, marketing will become something that you quite like doing – yes, really – and that you can easily fit into your busy schedule of looking after your clients and doing what you really love.

Enjoy your journey!

I Can't Write A Book!

- 🍏 I don't know what to write about!

- 🍏 Who will read what I want to write?

- 🍏 I don't know where to start!

I hear these phrases a lot from coaches, consultants and trainers. I always knew that I wanted to write a book and for a long time I didn't know where to start. This is actually the second book I started writing and now it's done, I can go back and finish the first one. This one came about because I was asked to give a presentation to a group of consultants on Marketing Planning. To write the presentation, I went back to the SOS Marketing Plan and created a talk around a number of the sections. Suddenly I realised that I had a ready-made structure for this book. And that is one of the secrets of writing a book – get the structure sorted and you'll have your starting place. Once you have this, the copy will start to flow.

Will people want to read what you write? If you have a business and clients who come to you for advice, then there will people out there who want to read what you write!

So how do you get the structure? That can be the tricky bit! What you need is someone who can help you get all your thoughts and ideas out of your head and onto paper, or flip charts. You need someone who can take you through that process, who can turn all your ideas into a structure, with chapters and sections; someone who can mentor you through the writing, supporting you along the way.

Once you've written your book, you then need someone to help you create the actual book, someone who can do the arty stuff and make it look great. Finally, you need someone to help you promote your book and sell it to your waiting audience.

At Appletree Publications we help our clients to work through that process. We take you from an idea about writing a book, to a finished product you will be proud of, that will help you grow your business. Get in touch to find out how we can help you turn your idea into a great book.

Apple tree
Publications

Call: 01635 578 500

Email: Admin@Appletreeuk.com

Website: www.Appletreeuk.com